MW00584097

All My Love.
Mxxx.
2013.

INSPIRATION

FOR

MUSICIANS

INSPIRATION FOR MUSICIANS

Copyright © Summersdale Publishers Ltd, 2012

All rights reserved.

No part of this book may be reproduced by any means, nor transmitted, nor translated into a machine language, without the written permission of the publishers.

Condition of Sale
This book is sold subject to the condition that it shall not, by way of trade or otherwise, be lent, re-sold, hired out or otherwise circulated in any form of binding or cover other than that in which it is published and without a similar condition including this condition being imposed on the subsequent publisher.

Summersdale Publishers Ltd
46 West Street
Chichester
West Sussex
PO19 1RP
UK

www.summersdale.com

Printed and bound in the Czech Republic

ISBN: 978-1-84953-216-7

Substantial discounts on bulk quantities of Summersdale books are available to corporations, professional associations and other organisations. For details telephone Summersdale Publishers on (+44-1243-771107), fax (+44-1243-786300) or email (nicky@summersdale.com).

INSPIRATION

FOR

MUSICIANS

EMILY DARCY

summersdale

Without music,
life would be a mistake.

FRIEDRICH NIETZSCHE

I can only think of music as
something inherent in every
human being – birthright.
Music coordinates mind,
body and spirit.

YEHUDI MENUHIN

Music doesn't lie. If there is something to be changed in this world, then it can only happen through music.

JIMI HENDRIX

Sounds like the blues are
composed of feeling,
finesse and fear.

BILLY GIBBONS

Music is the space
between the notes.

CLAUDE DEBUSSY

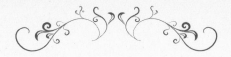

First you master your
instrument, then you master
the music; then you forget
about all that and just play.

CHARLIE PARKER

Music, being identical with heaven, isn't a thing of momentary thrills, or even hourly ones. It's a condition of eternity.

GUSTAV HOLST

All deep things are Song.
It seems somehow the very
central essence of us, Song;
as if all the rest were but
wrappages and hulls!

THOMAS CARLYLE

Music is an outburst
of the soul.

FREDERICK DELIUS

The symphony must be
like the world. It must
embrace everything.

GUSTAV MAHLER

I've never known a musician
who regretted being one.

VIRGIL THOMSON

Bach opens a vista to the universe. After experiencing him, people feel there is meaning to life after all.

Helmut Walcha

Percussion is like walking
through the forest. You can't
possibly see it all, there are
endless possibilities of
what you can do.

JOHN BERGAMO

Music, when soft voices die,
Vibrates in the memory.

PERCY BYSSHE SHELLEY,
'MUSIC, WHEN SOFT
VOICES DIE'

Sing lustily and with good courage. Beware of singing as if you were half dead, or half asleep; but lift up your voice with strength.

JOHN WESLEY

A great song should destroy
cop cars and set fire to the
suburbs. I'm only interested
in writing great songs.

TOM MORELLO

I have always believed that
opera is a planet where the
muses work together, join
hands and celebrate
all the arts.

FRANCO ZEFFIRELLI

I would teach children music,
physics and philosophy; but
most importantly music, for
in the patterns of music and
all the arts are the keys
of learning.

PLATO

Alas for those that
never sing,
But die with all their music
in them!

OLIVER WENDELL HOLMES
SR, 'THE VOICELESS'

Rock's so good to me.
Rock is my child and
my grandfather.

CHUCK BERRY

Learning music by reading
about it is like making
love by mail.

LUCIANO PAVAROTTI

I sing like I feel.

ELLA FITZGERALD

The piano is able to
communicate the subtlest
universal truths by means
of wood, metal and
vibrating air.

KENNETH MILLER

Virtue is the strong stem of man's nature, and music is the blossoming of virtue.

CONFUCIUS

My heart, which is so full to overflowing, has often been solaced and refreshed by music when sick and weary.

MARTIN LUTHER

Guitar playing is a release,
liberation. Put simply
it is freedom.

WILLIAM CHRISTOPHER
HANDY

Music is the shorthand
of emotion.

LEO TOLSTOY

I hate complacency. I play
every gig as if it could be
my last, then I enjoy it
more than ever.

NIGEL KENNEDY

… you are the music
While the music lasts.

T. S. Eliot,
'The Dry Salvages'

Don't play what's there.
Play what's not there.

MILES DAVIS

In order to compose, all you
need to do is remember a
tune that nobody else has
thought of.

ROBERT SCHUMANN

To stop the flow of music
would be like the stopping
of time itself, incredible
and inconceivable.

AARON COPLAND

Music is the language
spoken by angels.

HENRY WADSWORTH
LONGFELLOW

What have I got? No looks,
no money, no education.
Just talent.

SAMMY DAVIS JR

Music expresses that which
cannot be said and on which
it is impossible to be silent.

VICTOR HUGO

It's easy to play any musical instrument: all you have to do is touch the right key at the right time and the instrument will play itself.

JOHANN SEBASTIAN BACH

… there is no feeling, perhaps, except the extremes of fear and grief, that does not find relief in music.

GEORGE ELIOT,
THE MILL ON THE FLOSS

Seemed to me that
drumming was the best way
to get close to God.

LIONEL HAMPTON

The music soars within
the little lark,
And the lark soars.

ELIZABETH BARRETT
BROWNING, *AURORA LEIGH*

Rock 'n' roll: music for
the neck downwards.

KEITH RICHARDS

I think music in itself is
healing. It's an explosive
expression of humanity.
It's something we are all
touched by.

BILLY JOEL

What passion cannot music
raise and quell?

JOHN DRYDEN, 'A SONG FOR
ST. CECILIA'S DAY'

I'm an interpreter of stories
and when I perform it's like
I'm just sitting down at my
piano and telling
fairy stories.

NAT KING COLE

After silence, that which
comes nearest to expressing
the inexpressible is music.

ALDOUS HUXLEY,
MUSIC AT NIGHT

All good music resembles
something. Good music
stirs by its mysterious
resemblance to the objects
and feelings which
motivated it.

JEAN COCTEAU

We are the music makers,
And we are the dreamers
of dreams.

ARTHUR O'SHAUGHNESSY,
'ODE'

Music is a moral law. It
gives soul to the universe,
wings to the mind, flight to
the imagination, a charm to
sadness, gaiety and life
to everything.

PLATO

Music can change the
world because it can
change people.

BONO

Music is forever; music
should grow and mature
with you, following you
right on up until you die.

PAUL SIMON

Music washes away
from the soul the dust
of everyday life.

BERTHOLD AUERBACH

If I were to begin life again,
I would devote it to music.
It is the only cheap and
unpunished rapture
upon earth.

SYDNEY SMITH

Music is the wine which inspires one to new generative processes, and I am the Bacchus who presses out this glorious wine for mankind and makes them spiritually drunken.

LUDWIG VAN BEETHOVEN

… he who sings scares
away his woes.

MIGUEL DE CERVANTES,
DON QUIXOTE

The day you open your
mind to music, you're
halfway to opening your
mind to life.

PETE TOWNSHEND

Music is enough for a
lifetime – but a lifetime is
not enough for music.

Sergei Rachmaninov

Music is what life
sounds like.

ERIC OLSON

Truly there would be
reason to go mad were it
not for music.

PYOTR ILYICH TCHAIKOVSKY

Music produces a kind of
pleasure which human
nature cannot do without.

CONFUCIUS

I did think I did see all
Heaven before me, and the
great God himself.

GEORGE FRIDERIC HANDEL,
ON COMPOSING *MESSIAH*

Music is the voice that tells
us that the human race is
greater than it knows.

Napoleon Bonaparte

The best music…
[is] essentially there to
provide you something to
face the world with.

BRUCE SPRINGSTEEN

I have no pleasure in any man who despises music. It is no invention of ours: it is a gift of God.

MARTIN LUTHER

I am in the world only for
the purpose of composing.

FRANZ SCHUBERT

Where words fail,
music speaks.

HANS CHRISTIAN ANDERSEN

Music is the mediator
between the spiritual and
the sensual life.

LUDWIG VAN BEETHOVEN

Music is the art which
is most nigh to tears
and memory.

Oscar Wilde

Music helps you find the
truths you must bring into
the rest of your life.

ALANIS MORISSETTE

Such sweet compulsion
doth in music lie…

JOHN MILTON

Jazz is not dead,
it just smells funny.

FRANK ZAPPA

Take a music-bath once
or twice a week for a few
seasons, and you will find
that it is to the soul what the
water-bath is to the body.

OLIVER WENDELL
HOLMES SR

Great art is as irrational as
great music. It is mad with
its own loveliness.

GEORGE JEAN NATHAN

What we play is life.

LOUIS ARMSTRONG

If music be the food of love,
play on;
Give me excess of it.

WILLIAM SHAKESPEARE,
TWELFTH NIGHT

A musician's or artist's
responsibility is a simple
one, and that is, through
your music to tell the truth.

TOM MORELLO

Music, once admitted to
the soul, becomes a sort of
spirit, and never dies.

EDWARD GEORGE
BULWER-LYTTON

Music can bring a tear to your eye. It can make you jump out of your seat and applaud, and that's why we're here.

HAROLD WHEELER

A jazz musician is a
juggler who uses harmonies
instead of oranges.

BENNY GREEN

When words leave off,
music begins.

HEINRICH HEINE

Technically, I'm not even
a guitar player; all I play is
truth and emotion.

JIMI HENDRIX

Let me have music dying,
and I seek
No more delight.

JOHN KEATS, 'ENDYMION'

The blues tells a story.
Every line of the blues
has a meaning.

JOHN LEE HOOKER

Music is the language of the
spirit. It opens the secret
of life, bringing peace,
abolishing strife.

KHALIL GIBRAN

I pay no attention whatever
to anybody's praise or
blame. I simply follow
my own feelings.

WOLFGANG AMADEUS
MOZART

If I were not a physicist,
I would probably be a
musician... I see my life in
terms of music.

ALBERT EINSTEIN

Country music is three
chords and the truth.

HARLAN HOWARD

To send light into the
darkness of men's hearts –
such is the duty of the artist.

ROBERT SCHUMANN

Let me write the songs of a nation and I care not who writes the laws.

PLATO

The history of a people is
found in its songs.

GEORGE JELLINEK

A painter paints his pictures
on canvas. But musicians
paint their pictures
on silence.

LEOPOLD STOKOWSKI

If you can walk you can
dance. If you can talk
you can sing.

ZIMBABWEAN PROVERB

INSPIRATION
FOR
WRITERS

ISBN: 978-1-84953-214-3

Hardback

£4.99

'If there is a book you want to read but it hasn't been written yet, then you must write it.'

Toni Morrison

Believe it or not, even the greatest literary heavyweights suffer from writer's block sometimes. This little book, filled with the wit and wisdom of some of the most renowned authors of all time, is sure to provide inspiration and help those words keep flowing!

INSPIRATION
FOR
ARTISTS

ISBN: 978-1-84953-215-0

Hardback

£4.99

d is an artist. The problem is how to
in an artist once we grow up.'

Pablo Picasso

t a picture paints a thousand words, but
ven the most creative people need help to
stic juices flowing. This little book, filled
and wisdom of some of the world's most
inters, sculptors and other visual artists, is
le inspiration for all who make the world a
e beautiful place through their art.

If you're interested in finding
more about our gift books, foll
on Twitter: **@Summersd**

www.summersdale.